TO

Debbie & Paul,   Debbie & Paul

WATERWAYS
Past & Present

with love from.

Bec
x

Ian

Sophie

Mike

DEREK PRATT

WATERWAYS
Past & Present

A UNIQUE PORTRAIT OF BRITAIN'S WATERWAYS HERITAGE

ADLARD COLES NAUTICAL

BLOOMSBURY
LONDON · NEW DELHI · NEW YORK · SYDNEY

Adlard Coles Nautical
An imprint of Bloomsbury Publishing Plc

50 Bedford Square   1385 Broadway
London   New York
WC1B 3DP   NY 10018
UK   USA

www.bloomsbury.com

ADLARD COLES, ADLARD COLES NAUTICAL
and the Buoy logo are trademarks of
Bloomsbury Publishing Plc

First published in 2006
Reprinted 2007 and 2008
Second edition 2015

British Library Cataloguing-in-Publication Data
A catalogue record for this book is available from the British Library.

Library of Congress Cataloguing-in-Publication data has been applied for.

ISBN 978-1-4729-1201-5
ePDF 978-1-4729-1266-4
ePub 978-1-4729-1265-7

2 4 6 8 10 9 7 5 3 1

Typeset in 9.5 on 13pt ITC New Baskerville by Susan McIntyre.
Printed and bound in China by RRD South China

Bloomsbury Publishing Plc makes every effort to ensure that the papers
used in the manufacture of our books are natural, recyclable products made
from wood grown in well-managed forests. Our manufacturing processes
conform to the environmental regulations of the country of origin.

To find out more about our authors and books visit www.bloomsbury.com.
Here you will find extracts, author interviews, details of forthcoming events
and the option to sign up for our newsletters.

Contents

Introduction: Times of Change

The second half of the 18th century was a time of change throughout the world. In France and America this manifested itself in bloody revolutions, but in Britain a more peaceful change took place. It became known as the Industrial Revolution, and it was the canals that made it all possible. Led by engineers like James Brindley and financed by businessmen like Josiah Wedgwood, they connected the main rivers and ports with artificial waterways.

A second wave of canal building came during the first quarter of the 19th century. Thomas Telford and his contemporaries had learned the lessons of James Brindley and the pioneer canal builders which were to keep the new canals in a straight line and avoid the earlier meandering, contour hugging waterways. The new canals had deep cuttings and embankments keeping locks bunched together in long flights. Journeys on the older canals were too slow when economic pressure demanded a fast delivery of cargoes.

The Stockton and Darlington Railway opened in 1825 heralding a warning to all inland waterborne transport. Railways were built throughout the country with the same enthusiasm and speculation that had greeted the height of canal building fifty years earlier. The railways didn't have summertime water problems and could still operate in freezing conditions. They could also handle bulk cargoes and were quicker.

During this period the boating families were forced to leave their canalside cottages and move into the cramped boat cabins. The new aggressive competitor meant that costs had to be cut and the boatman could no longer afford to live ashore. An indigenous floating population developed with their own traditions, that lasted over a hundred years. That period of time saw the slow decline of commercial carrying on most of the canals, with some of them gradually becoming uneconomic and forced to close.

This situation was often accelerated by the purchase of canals by railway companies who then allowed their watery competitors to decline through lack of maintenance.

The boating families who toiled up and down the English canals in 1850 would have still recognised most of the familiar places if a time machine could have propelled them into the mid-20th century. The fabric of the waterways remained constant with its mills and warehouses, wharves and factories. The bridges, locks, tunnels and aqueducts were still there although motorboats had replaced traditional horse-power.

By 1960, the first motorways had made their appearance and the railways began to suffer the kind of competition they had inflicted on the canals over a hundred years earlier. The severe winter of 1962–1963 finally brought an end to regular commercial carrying on the narrow canals.

Project the boatman from 1850 to the start of the 21st century and he would be bewildered to see the changes in his former working environment. The Victorian warehouses and mills have either been demolished or transformed into offices and apartments. New bridges cross the waterways with the cacophony of modern motor transport, and pleasure boats fill the locks and line the banks. Place him at Old Turn Junction or Gas Street Basin in the centre of Birmingham, and he would struggle to find anything recognisable. The same would apply at Paddington Basin or the former Brentford Dock in London. Regent's Canal Dock is now Limehouse Basin, filled with pleasure boats and housing for City workers. Today there are Brindley Houses, James Brindley pubs, Telford Way, Narrowboat Way and Boathorse Hill. All these names refer to new roads, housing developments and commercial science parks, recalling the men who built the canals and worked upon them all those years ago.

LEFT Caen Hill Locks, Devizes, Kennet and Avon Canal.

PART ONE

The Age of Brindley

Was James Brindley the greatest canal engineer? Waterway historians and writers point to the achievements of such worthies as William Jessop, John Rennie and Thomas Telford. All were great men in their time, but Brindley was the pioneer canal engineer whose example was set for all his successors to learn from. When Brindley built Harecastle Tunnel it was the first time anyone had attempted such a monumental feat of engineering. He encountered numerous geological obstacles that took years to overcome, but in the end he succeeded. When Telford built his adjacent tunnel fifty years later, most of the problems had been solved and he also had the advantage of more modern surveying methods and civil engineering techniques.

BELOW The Packet House at Worsley. A passenger service began from here to Manchester in 1766, bringing in additional revenue for the Duke of Bridgewater. The entrance to the Duke's mines can be found beyond the bridge in the background.

ABOVE Statue of James Brindley at Etruria, Stoke-on-Trent.

BELOW Brindley is remembered by this street name in Birmingham.

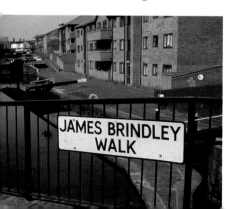

The Bridgewater Canal

The canal age began in 1765 with the completion of the Duke of Bridgewater's Canal, which connected the Duke's coal mines at Worsley to the centre of Manchester. The contoured canal was lock-free but the engineers, John Gilbert and James Brindley, faced the problem of crossing the River Irwell. They solved this by constructing a stone aqueduct at Barton which was 200 yards long and 38 feet above the river. This was a considerable achievement at that time and attracted huge crowds to witness its opening in 1761. The aqueduct stayed in use until 1893 when it was replaced by the present Barton Swing Aqueduct over the Manchester Ship Canal.

ABOVE Statue of Josiah Wedgwood (1730–1795) outside the Wedgwood Visitor Centre at Barlaston near Stoke-on-Trent. He was the chief sponsor for Brindley's Trent and Mersey Canal and built his first ceramics factory by the canal at Etruria.

LEFT The entrance to the Duke's mines at Worsley. Inside the mines were about 46 miles of subterranean canal connected by inclined planes. Women and children were employed inside the mines in conditions that were described as horrific. Only the entrance can be seen today, with the water stained orange because of seepage from inside the mine.

The Trent and Mersey Canal

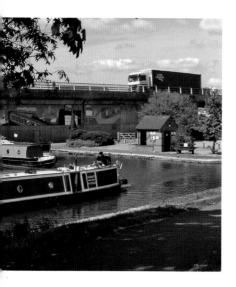

Burton-upon-Trent has become universally famous for its production of beer, and many of Britain's main breweries are still located in the town. Like the pottery industry around Stoke, Burton's brewing industry owes much of its success to the Trent and Mersey Canal. Horninglow Wharf was the dividing point where the canal changed from being a wide beamed waterway to a narrow one. The wide canal enabled barges to reach Burton and carry the produce of the brewing industry to Hull for export to Europe and beyond.

The Trent and Mersey Canal was the first important long distance artificial waterway in Britain. Originally called the Grand Trunk Canal, it made the first inland waterway connection between the North Sea and the Irish Sea. It runs from Shardlow on the River Trent to Preston Brook by the River Mersey where it connects to the Duke of Bridgewater's Canal. Completed in 1777 after eleven years work, it has wide barge size locks at each end but narrow locks in the centre. This set the seven-foot standard gauge for most of Brindley's network of canals. The Trent and Mersey was the start of Brindley's vision of a Grand Cross of canals that eventually would connect the ports of the Humber, Mersey, Severn and Thames with the emerging industrial heartland of the Midlands.

ABOVE AND RIGHT The black and white photo shows a very run-down Horninglow Wharf in April 1976 with a wide-beamed hotel boat in the foreground being painted for the coming season. In the background, the overhanging salt warehouse and its attendant buildings have all been demolished, as is evident by the colour photo taken in 2005 (both photos taken from the same position).

OPPOSITE At the eastern end of the Trent and Mersey Canal is Brindley's inland port at Shardlow. Although no longer an active port, it is now a busy boating centre with boatyards and marinas. Many of the original buildings have survived and have been converted to new uses. The building in the background of the photograph is the Clock Warehouse which once handled goods underneath a loading arch. It is now a popular pub and restaurant.

The banks of the Trent and Mersey Canal through Stoke-on-Trent were lined with the distinctive bottle kilns used in the pottery industry. There were over 2,000 of these kilns throughout the Potteries, creating fine porcelain and ceramics. Working within these ovens was an arduous task, especially for the boys known as 'sagger maker's bottom-knockers' who worked long hours at the base of the hot kilns. A sagger was a round fireclay box that held ware during firing in the bottle oven and the bottom knocker was an assistant to the sagger maker. Most of the canalside bottle kilns have gone, leaving these two examples at Hanley that stand forlorn amid the ruins of the factory they once served night and day.

ABOVE The author Arnold Bennett (1867–1931) was born in Hanley and would probably have recognised this row of canal workers' houses. Bennett was a descendant of James Brindley, following the great engineer's affair with Mary Bennett five years before his marriage to Anne Henshall in 1765. Brindley's illegitimate son John was the great-grandfather of the Five Town's novelist. Photographed on a bleak winter's day in January 1973, this row of canalside houses has since been demolished and replaced by modern housing.

RIGHT Bottle kilns by Trent and Mersey Canal at Stoke-on-Trent.

It took eleven years to complete Harecastle Tunnel, by which time Brindley had died through diabetes and overwork. Once open, the canal was extremely busy and the narrow tunnel soon became a bottleneck. Thomas Telford's adjacent tunnel, built in 1827, allowed traffic to run in both directions until Brindley's tunnel finally collapsed through subsidence. Telford's 3,000 yard tunnel is still used today under strict control by tunnel-keepers at each end. The entrance to Brindley's tunnel can be seen to the right of the one used now. The orange staining in the water is caused by iron ore seepage from mines within Brindley's tunnel.

BELOW Harecastle Tunnel.

Joule's Brewery was built in Stone in 1758, 13 years before Brindley's Trent and Mersey Canal arrived in the town. The 'Stone Ale' brewed here was exported throughout the world. Alfred Barnard wrote in 1889, 'Who has not heard of Stone Ale, that ancient and wholesome beverage, whose praises have been lauded in prose and song for almost 150 years.'

Today, Stone announces itself as 'The Canal Town' where there are locks and several boatyards close to the town centre.

ABOVE The old brewery at Stone seen on a frosty winter's morning.

RIGHT Originally a slaughterhouse, the Star Inn at Stone became a pub in 1568, predating the canal by two hundred years. In 1940, the citizens of Stone clubbed together and raised £5,000 to build a Spitfire. The plane was named Star of Stone after the pub.

The Caldon Canal

The Caldon Canal was built to bring limestone from the hills around Cauldon Low to use in the pottery industry at Stoke-on-Trent. It is a branch of the Trent and Mersey with a junction at Etruria near to the original Wedgwood factory. In its early stages the canal is intensely built-up, but once clear of the Potteries' urban sprawl it becomes one of the most picturesque and remote canals on the inland waterway system. The Caldon Canal splits at Hazelhurst, with one branch going to Leek and the other to Froghall, where it once connected to the now derelict Uttoxeter Canal. It was during the surveying for the Caldon Canal that Brindley caught a cold and became seriously ill. This led to his death in 1772 from diabetes and overwork.

BELOW The Leek Branch of the Caldon Canal at Hazelhurst. This is moorland scenery at its finest and just a few miles from Stoke-on-Trent. The boat in the picture has just crossed an unusual aqueduct, where one branch of the canal crosses over the other.

The Caldon Canal was closed to navigation in 1961 and could have been lost forever. Its eventual restoration in 1974 was mostly due to the endeavours of volunteers from the Caldon Canal Society and funding from local councils. Cheddleton Flint Mill by the Caldon Canal was where flint was ground for use in the pottery and ceramic industry. Powdered flint used to whiten pottery was carried by canal to the factories. The ground, calcinated flints were an important part of Josiah Wedgwood's new product called 'creamware'. Being white, calcinated flint was an excellent ingredient in the light-coloured pottery that had become popular at the time. The calcination kilns, where flints were heated to make them brittle, can be seen next to the towpath. Two undershot water wheels that drove the grinding machinery still operate on open days. Today, the mills and waterwheels are run by volunteers and are open to the public at weekends.

ABOVE Work in progress restoring Cheddleton Lock in September 1973.

RIGHT Cheddleton Flint Mill by the Caldon Canal.

Jesse Shirley's Etruscan Bone and Flint Mill is situated at Etruria Junction where the Caldon Canal meets the Trent and Mersey. It was built in 1857 to grind bone and flint for the pottery industry. Now the Etruria Industrial Museum, it retains most of its original machinery and has one of the oldest working steam engines in the country.

ABOVE Jesse Shirley's Mill at Etruria Junction. Since this photograph was taken in 1995, a modern extension to the museum has been erected behind the mill on the bank of the Caldon Canal opposite a statue of James Brindley.

Consall Forge by the Caldon Canal in the Churnet Valley is difficult to find by road. Walk the towpath from Froghall or travel by boat and you find a remote pub, a steam railway and superb scenery. Only the limekilns remain as reminders of Consall Forge's industrial past when it was the centre of the red ironstone industry. In its commercial heyday, boats loaded with ironstone and limestone from the hills beyond Froghall would have streamed past Consall Forge in great numbers. The Cherry Eye Mines closed in 1923, leaving a legacy in the name 'Cherry Eye Bridge'. The bridge has an unusual Gothic arch and can be seen between Consall Forge and Froghall.

ABOVE Cherry Eye Bridge near Froghall.

RIGHT Consall Forge.

The Staffs and Worcester Canal

The Staffs and Worcester Canal connects the Trent and Mersey Canal at Great Haywood near Stafford to the River Severn at Stourport. The canal passes through the centre of Kidderminster, but apart from that manages to avoid built-up areas. It is a delightfully rural canal for much of its 46-mile length, despite never being very far from the Black Country. At Stourport, Brindley created a magnificent inland port with a series of basins now used as moorings for a miscellany of river and canal craft.

Great Haywood has a beautiful setting at the edge of Cannock Chase and is close to Shugborough Hall. Tixall Wide, a nearby ornamental lake that incorporates the canal, was created to appease the local Lord of the Manor.

BELOW The sinuous lines of Great Haywood Junction Bridge mark the junction of Brindley's Trent and Mersey and Staffs and Worcester Canals.

Bratch Locks on the Staffs and Worcester Canal can be confusing to inexperienced boaters. To all outward appearances they look like interconnected staircase locks, when in fact they are actually separated by a short pound. The three locks are topped by an elegant octagonal toll house where a lock keeper helps boaters solve the mysteries of negotiating the locks. For years the toll house and its surroundings were whitewashed, as seen in the black and white photo taken in 1975 (left). Since then the entire area has been restored to its original brick and the lockside has been improved – see the photo below taken in 2014.

LEFT St Mary's parish church overlooks the Staffs and Worcester Canal at Kidderminster. Carpet factories used to flank the canal, but sadly most of them have been converted to new uses or demolished in favour of supermarkets. Kidderminster has been a carpet centre since 1735 and had a boom period as recent as the 1960s. Unfortunately the carpet industry in the town has gone into sharp decline over the last few years. High sandstone cliffs edge the canal in a beautiful wooded section just south of the town centre.

Brindley's inland port at Stourport is at the southern end of the Staffs and Worcester Canal. There was nothing at Stourport before Brindley arrived with his canal in 1766. By 1783 there were brass and iron foundries, a vinegar brewery, spinning mills, carpet factories, boat builders, warehouses, shops and inns. Several canal basins were constructed at different levels connected by locks. The Clock Warehouse, topped by a clock made in 1813, overlooks the Upper Basin. Here too is the 100-room Tontine Hotel built at the time of the canal for visiting merchants. With its position by the River Severn, Stourport has become an inland resort with a variety of pubs and restaurants, and even has a permanent funfair.

LEFT Colourful boats in Stourport Basin.

BELOW The Clock Warehouse at Stourport.

The Coventry Canal

The Coventry Canal has a chequered history. It was originally conceived to connect the Trent and Mersey Canal at Fradley to the Oxford Canal and then on to the River Thames. In doing so it would pass through the rich Warwickshire coalfield, providing Coventry with cheap coal. That section between Coventry and the coalfield was completed by 1769, but by 1771 the money had run out and the canal was still a long way from its northern objective. In the ensuing wrangles James Brindley was sacked. Finally the missing link was built as a joint venture by the Trent and Mersey Canal Company and the Birmingham and Fazeley Canal Company, whose canal had recently reached Fazeley. The Coventry Canal Company later bought this section back but even today some maps still refer to the section between Fazeley and Whittington as the Birmingham and Fazeley Canal.

ABOVE Hawkesbury, on the northern outskirts of Coventry, is at the junction of the Oxford and Coventry Canals. Known as Sutton Stop, the junction has long been a meeting place for working boats. It was close to the collieries, had a boatman's pub and facilities for boating families. For some years the Coventry and Oxford Canals ran side by side and remained unconnected because of disputes between the two canal companies. The addition of new housing has visibly changed the junction, but the old pumping station and elegant bridge remain.

ABOVE Working boats moored on the Coventry Canal near Hawkesbury Junction towards the end of the 1960s. These were the remnants of the coal carrying fleets of narrowboats that worked from the local collieries. By now most of the boating families were struggling to make a living.

RIGHT Joe and Rose Skinner aboard their narrowboat *Friendship* at Sutton Stop, Hawkesbury Junction in February 1974.

ABOVE A pair of working boats on the Coventry Canal in 1958. The lady steering the unpowered butty boat is being towed by her husband on the motor boat. These loaded coal boats were probably en route to a factory in the south.

Joe Skinner was the last of the 'Number One' owner boaters working on the Midland canals and one of the last working boatmen to work with a horse in preference to a motor boat. They were retired when the photo shown below was taken, and although they had a cottage nearby they chose to spend most of the day on their boat. *Friendship* has been restored and is now exhibited at the Ellesmere Port Boat Museum.

ABOVE Information boards have been produced for the large Asian population that live alongside the Coventry Canal in the north part of the city. This one explains the importance of water in the Hindu religion.

RIGHT Cash's Top Shops, alongside the Coventry Canal.

Cash's Top Shops on the Coventry Canal are about half a mile from the terminal basin. Weavers lived in houses below the factory on the top floor which was a continuous workshop with steam driven looms running the whole length of the row. The workers only had to climb upstairs to start their day's work. The Top Shops, which were built in 1857, produced name-tapes that identified school clothes for children, and work clothing for adults.

The Oxford Canal

Brindley's Grand Cross of canals was completed eighteen years after his death, when the Oxford Canal finally reached its destination with the River Thames at Oxford in 1790. The original canal between Hawkesbury Junction and Oxford was 90 miles long, but Brindley's meandering, contour-hugging waterway led to severe bottlenecks and time-wasting when the canal was busy. To speed up trade, fourteen miles was lopped off the northern section above Braunston during the 1930s by straightening out the loops with a new canal. The winding southern section remained the same and is today one of the most popular cruising waterways in the country.

LEFT Napton Locks on the Oxford Canal. The canal blends in so perfectly with the landscape it is hard to believe you are looking at an artificial waterway. Some changes have been made next to the lock since this photograph was taken in 1974, but mostly this timeless scene remains unspoilt.

OPPOSITE The windmill on Napton Hill overlooks Napton Locks and the Oxford Canal. The first windmill on Napton Hill was built in the middle of the 16th century. Clay was moved by boat from the extensive quarries that bit into the hillside. There is a beautiful view of the surrounding countryside from beneath the windmill.

On the 29th June 1644 a furious Civil War battle took place at Cropredy Bridge between Cromwell's army and a Royalist force. Both factions were well matched, each with around 9,000 men on horse or on foot. A plaque on the river bridge commemorates the battle. In more recent times, Cropredy has been host to the Fairport Convention Music Festival that takes place on the second weekend in August, attracting 20,000 music fans.

ABOVE The village church at Shipton-on-Cherwell predates the Oxford Canal by several centuries. This charming village is just a few miles north of Oxford close to Woodstock and Blenheim Palace, birthplace of Sir Winston Churchill.

On Christmas Eve 1874 there was a railway accident when a crowded train left the nearby track and fell into the canal, 34 people were killed and 64 injured.

RIGHT Cropredy Lock on the Oxford Canal.

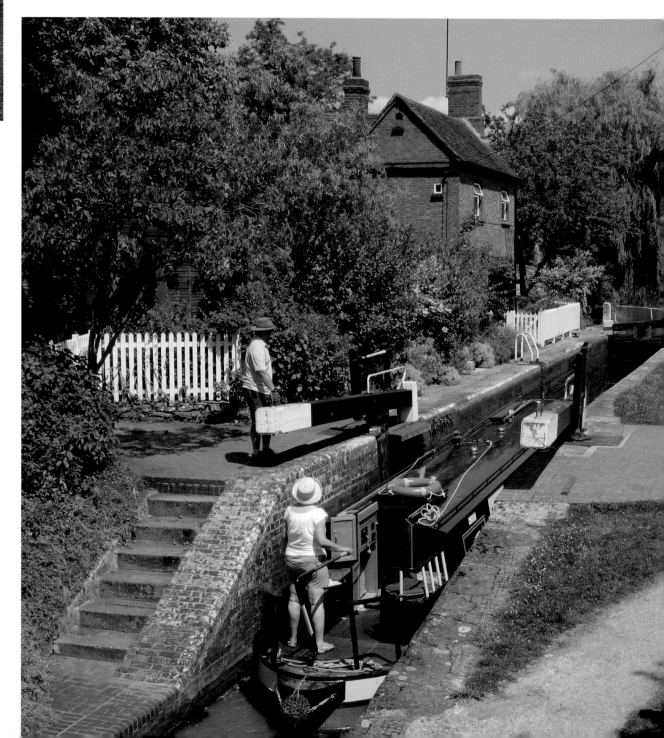

The section of the Oxford Canal between Braunston and Napton Junction is shared with the Grand Union Canal. Braunston, because of its carrying companies and boatyards, became a place where working boat families congregated and bought supplies. Braunston church was where they often married and buried their dead. Many of the old working boats and their traditions can be seen at an annual boat rally parade at Braunston.

BELOW Narrowboats on the Oxford Canal at Braunston near the junction with the Grand Union Canal.

The Chesterfield Canal

Whitsunday Pie Lock has achieved fame because of its extraordinary name. Legend has it that a local farmer's wife baked a pie for the navvies on completion of building the lock on a Whitsunday. However, recent research has concluded the story as apocryphal, the name originating from Old English 'pightie' meaning enclosure and the Whitsunday from a tenancy change on that day. Nevertheless, Retford & Worksop Boat Club celebrate the legend by sharing a pie by the lockside every Whitsunday.

ABOVE The black and white photo shows the Pickford's Warehouse at Worksop on the Chesterfield Canal in June 1973. Boats using the covered arch could load and unload directly from the warehouse.

ABOVE AND RIGHT Whitsunday Pie Lock, the last broad gauge lock on the canal.

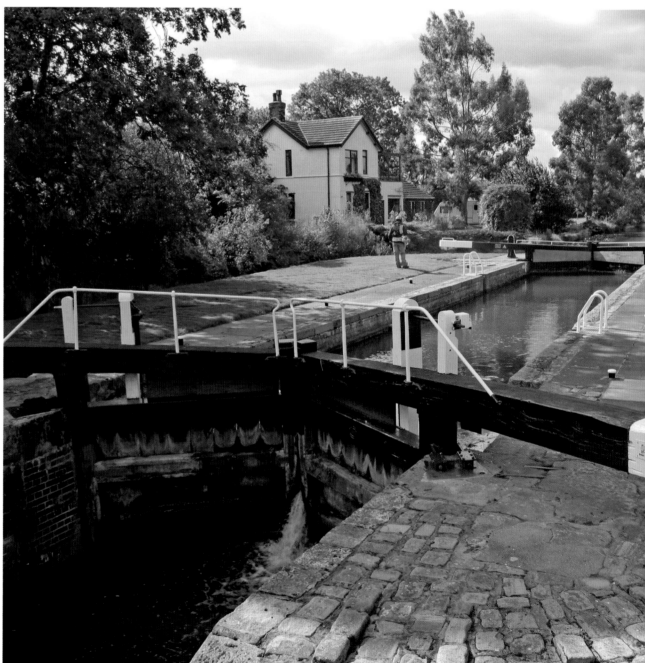

The Chesterfield Canal is an isolated waterway only connected to the rest of the system by the tidal River Trent. Originally surveyed by Brindley, construction of the 45-mile canal began in 1771 and took six years to complete. At first it was a very successful waterway, but the 3102-yard long Norwood Tunnel proved unstable from the outset. It was one of the longest canal tunnels ever built in Britain, and eventually had to be closed in 1907 after the roof collapsed. The canal fell into decline and the section between Worksop and Chesterfield became derelict. Only the efforts of volunteers and the Retford & Worksop Boat Club kept the rest of the canal open. The canal has been now been restored as far as Norwood Tunnel and work is progressing at the Chesterfield end.

BELOW The Chesterfield Canal at Cinderhill near Shireoaks. This beautiful section between Worksop and Norwood Tunnel has recently been restored after years of dereliction.

The Pennine Canals

'Among these dark Satanic mills.' WILLIAM BLAKE

Several of the mills by the Leeds and Liverpool Canal at Burnley, shown in the picture below, have since been demolished – one after a fire. Despite the loss, this section of canal in Burnley has become a heritage trail and is being promoted as the Weavers' Triangle. Burnley also has an impressive 60-foot high embankment that carries the canal across part of the town and is almost a mile in length.

BELOW The Leeds and Liverpool Canal at Burnley, photographed in May 1972.

Three canals cross the Pennine watershed. On each side of the hills they pass through old industrial towns whose prosperity was made in the wool and cotton trade. The canals enabled the mills to be supplied with essential raw materials and provided an outlet to the ports at Liverpool and Hull. Between them the three canals required 260 locks in various sizes to allow boats to pass over their summit levels in the high hills. One of the canals also needed the longest canal tunnel ever built in Britain at Standedge.

Two of the canals – the Rochdale Canal and the Huddersfield Narrow Canal – eventually succumbed to economic pressure. They were closed and became derelict. Only the Leeds and Liverpool Canal, which is the longest and the oldest of the three, managed to survive. The Rochdale and Huddersfield Canals have since been restored to full navigation.

The locks were hard work for working boatmen in bygone days, but the superb Pennine moorland scenery has become a great attraction for today's pleasure boaters.

ABOVE Greenberfield Top Lock on the Pennine section of the Leeds and Liverpool Canal. At 127 miles, the Leeds and Liverpool is the longest canal in Britain. On the Lancashire side it passes through old mill towns like Blackburn, Burnley and Wigan, with Bingley and Skipton on the Yorkshire side.

Bingley Five Rise Locks raise the Leeds and Liverpool Canal 60 feet by a series of staircase locks in which one chamber leads into the next without an intervening pound. This means that the top gates of the lower lock become the bottom gates of the one above. An attendant lock keeper is at hand to help confused boaters negotiate the flight.

Apart from the five staircase locks at Bingley, there are several groups of three staircase locks on the Yorkshire side of the Leeds and Liverpool Canal.

ABOVE Newlay Locks, near Bramley on the outskirts of Leeds, are attractively set in woodland by a country park.

RIGHT Bingley Five Rise Locks.

Daisyfield Mill by the Leeds and Liverpool Canal at Blackburn was built as a corn mill in 1870. In later years it was a wallpaper factory and has now been converted to offices. The canal in the Blackburn area was once flanked by mills with industries that included paper making, cotton, flour and oat crushing. Terraced houses built for mill workers still remain by the canal in many northern towns like Blackburn. Whole families including children as young as ten years old would work long hours in the mill at the bottom of the street.

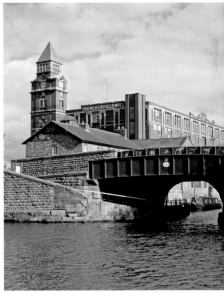

ABOVE Trencherfield Mill at Wigan once produced cotton but is now part of the 'Wigan Pier Heritage Experience'. It still has a massive working steam engine that once powered textile machines on five floors operating 97,000 spindles. This unlikely part of the Leeds and Liverpool Canal in Wigan has become a tourist attraction in the North West.

LEFT Daisyfield Mill at Blackburn.

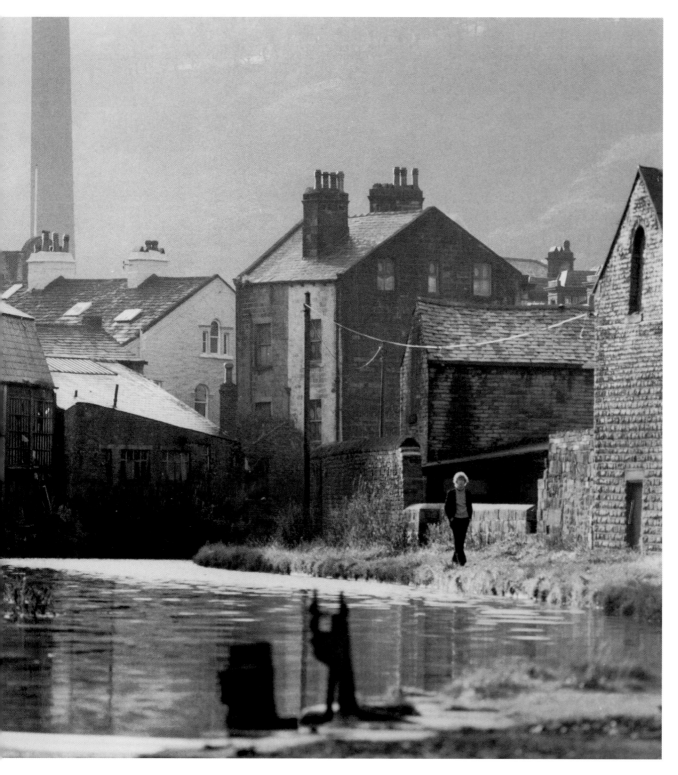

ABOVE A long flight of locks takes the Rochdale Canal through Todmorden up to the short summit level.

The Rochdale Canal in Todmorden is shown here when it was derelict in November 1973. The canal has since been restored but every building in this picture has been demolished. The Rochdale Canal was fully operational by 1804 which was seven years before its Huddersfield Narrow Canal neighbour. Commercially it was very successful because its broad locks allowed quite large vessels to cross the Pennine hills. Its problem lay in its very short summit level with inadequate water supplies to maintain busy traffic through 92 locks.

The section of the Rochdale Canal between Hebden Bridge and Todmorden passes through some of the most dramatic scenery to be found anywhere on England's canal system. Locks are frequent where canal, river, railway and road squeeze tightly together in a narrow wooded valley. Here at Lobb Mill energetic visitors can walk up to Stoodley Pike Monument that commemorates Napoleon's defeat at Waterloo.

ABOVE Youthful canoeists wait for the boat to pass at Lobb Mill, Rochdale Canal.

The last commercial boat to pass through the Rochdale Canal was narrowboat *Alice* carrying 20 tons of wire from Sowerby Bridge to Manchester in 1937. The canal became derelict, with bridges lowered and culverted and locks converted into weirs. There were plans to fill in several urban stretches which had become rubbish dumps. The first great clean up of the canal led by voluntary labour began in 1972 and the canal was finally reopened throughout in 2002.

RIGHT, TOP This picture of a derelict lock on the western side of the Rochdale Canal was taken in November 1973.

RIGHT The line of the Rochdale Canal just south of Rochdale had to be re-routed because of the nearby motorway. Consequently, a brand new lock had to be built. The picture shows the lock under construction in May 2002 only two months before the entire canal was officially reopened.

Tuel Lane Lock was opened in 1996 and replaced two derelict structures in the centre of Sowerby Bridge. It is almost 20 feet deep which makes it the deepest canal lock in the country. The lock is manned by a resident lock keeper so boaters should check times of operation.

A short tunnel under the main road was also required to reconnect the Rochdale Canal to the Calder and Hebble Navigation. Sowerby Bridge Basin has moorings and a boatyard surrounded by a collection of superb stone warehouses. Sowerby Bridge, with its numerous pubs and restaurants, makes an ideal stopping place for boaters attempting the South Pennine Cruising Ring.

LEFT Tuel Lane Lock on the Rochdale Canal.

Surrounded by high hills, Hebden Bridge epitomises the rugged, stone-built Northern mill town. The 'double-decker' houses that once housed mill workers can still be seen clinging to the steep hillside. Hebden Bridge and Heptonstall became prosperous for the production of corduroy and worsted textiles, and notorious in the mid-18th century for the Cragg Vale Coiners. Cragg Vale was an isolated village near Hebden Bridge where 'King' David Hartley and his gang of counterfeiters made gold coins of such quality that they went undetected for several years. The story ended in the betrayal of David Hartley and the murder of an Excise Officer. Hartley was hanged at York in April 1770 and is buried at Heptonstall.

Only 20 miles long, the Huddersfield Narrow Canal was the shortest of the Pennine canals. Even so there were still 74 narrow locks and Britain's longest canal tunnel to negotiate. The canal suffered from bad workmanship in its original construction, leaving it with flooding problems in later years. Not surprisingly these problems coupled with difficulties in negotiating Standedge Tunnel and competition from the railway brought the waterway into decline. It was abandoned after the Second World War but restored in 2001. Diggle Locks can be found on the western side of Standedge Tunnel as the canal descends through the Lancashire mill towns to Manchester.

ABOVE Diggle Locks on the Huddersfield Narrow Canal.

41

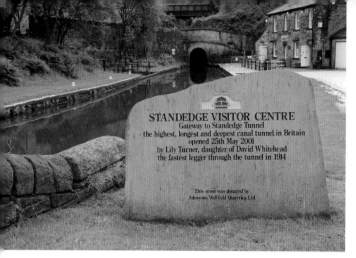

The entrance to Standedge Tunnel at Marsden looks like a mousehole underneath the towering Standedge Fell. At 5,415 feet it is by far the longest canal tunnel in Britain. In the days before powered boats, boatmen had to 'leg' the boats through the tunnel by 'walking' them along the tunnel wall, thereby pushing the boats through. The tunnel was restored to navigation in 2001 and now boats can pass through with an escorted passage which must be booked in advance.

LEFT AND BELOW Standedge Tunnel at Marsden.

Beneath this mill at Huddersfield is a bizarre lifting bridge called Locomotive Bridge that looks as if it was made out of Meccano pieces. The mill is close to the former transhipment basin where boats had to transfer cargoes from the wide Huddersfield Broad Canal to the Narrow Trans-Pennine waterway.

LEFT Locomotive Bridge at Huddersfield.

43

ABOVE Jack James photographed outside his cottage at Stoke Bruerne in June 1973. Mr James was a working boatman who later became a lock-keeper. His collection of waterway memorabilia was the foundation for the country's first Canal Museum at Stoke Bruerne. He died aged 78 in September 1974.

LEFT A pair of coal carrying narrowboats outside the Boat Inn at Stoke Bruerne in 1973. The interior of a narrowboat cabin was a masterpiece in the utilisation of space. Less than 7 feet wide, 9 feet long and under 6 feet high, boatmen's families would live, eat and sleep within these confines.

OPPOSITE Steam powered narrowboat *President* with butty boat *Kildare* in Stoke Bruerne Top Lock. The crew are dressed in traditional boatmen's clothes. The Canal Museum, housed in a former grain warehouse, can be seen by the trees in the background on the right of the picture.

The London Road

The London Road was the name given by working boatmen to the Grand Junction Canal. It was built between Braunston and the River Thames at Brentford as a quicker alternative route to London than the meandering, narrow locked Oxford Canal. It also avoided transhipment to Thames barges at Oxford followed by a long journey down river to London. The Grand Junction had wide locks, two long tunnels and an aqueduct over the River Great Ouse. It cut the previous journey by 60 miles.

A new route to Birmingham was established by the building of the Napton, Warwick and Birmingham Canals. Another connection to the Grand Junction was made to Leicester and then by the canalised River Soar to the Trent. All these waterways and their branches amalgamated in 1929 becoming the Grand Union Canal.

Braunston village is about two miles to the north west of Daventry in Northamptonshire, and is the hub of the inland waterway system south of Birmingham. Situated at the junction of the Grand Union and Oxford Canals, it has long been a gathering place for working narrowboats.

RIGHT Narrowboats at a working boat rally at Braunston.

BELOW Narrowboats *Alperton* and *Widgeon* carrying an experimental cargo of Massey Ferguson boxed tractor parts on the Grand Union Canal near Ivinghoe in February 1974. The boats went to Brentford where the cargo was loaded on to Thames lighters before being exported to South Africa from London Docks.

The daunting sight of 21 wide locks striding up the hillside at Hatton has made many a boatman quiver in his boots. It requires around 50,000 gallons of water to fill one of these Grand Union Canal locks, so a boat travelling up the flight releases a prodigious amount of water. Some water is saved by using the side pounds next to each lock which act as a reservoir. This view looking down the flight towards Warwick is taken from near the top of the locks.

RIGHT Hatton Bottom Lock, with its pretty lock cottage, is at the foot of the Hatton lock flight on the outskirts of Warwick.

Blisworth on the Grand Union Canal is the third longest navigable tunnel in Britain. It opened in 1805 and is wide enough for two narrowboats to pass each other inside. There is no towpath so boats had to be 'legged' through in the days before powered craft. Professional 'leggers' used to work boats through the tunnel – at a price! During the early 1980s the tunnel was closed because of structural problems and needed to be re-lined.

TOP RIGHT Work on the inside of the Blisworth tunnel in October 1983.

BOTTOM RIGHT A narrowboat enters the north end of Blisworth Tunnel. Waterproof clothing is recommended for steerers, especially after wet weather, as water pours down the ventilation shafts above the tunnel.

FAR RIGHT After miles of lock-free cruising, the ten staircase locks at Foxton can be a shock to the boater. They are arranged in two sets of five locks with a passing place between. In 1900 a steam-driven inclined plane was built to bypass the traffic bottleneck at Foxton Locks. It lasted only a few years before closing as it was expensive to operate and often broke down. Today, Foxton Locks are very popular with visitors who come to picnic and watch the boats.

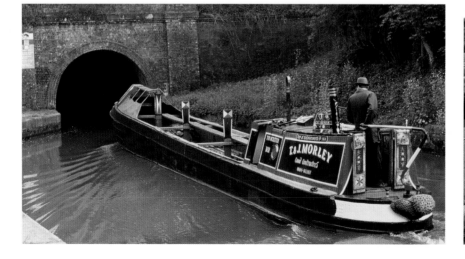

Crick is the beautiful setting for an annual boating festival at the end of May in a nearby marina. Cracks Hill, which was a Roman station, has superb views from its summit. Crick and its neighbour Husbands Bosworth both have long canal tunnels which were built in order to maintain a 20 mile level pound between the lock flights at Foxton and Watford (Northants).

ABOVE The Leicester branch of the Grand Union Canal at Crick.

LEFT In its southern section, the Leicester Canal meanders through peaceful farming countryside.

The London Canals

The Grand Junction Canal reached the Thames at Brentford in 1894 but was still some distance from the Docks and central London. The first canal to reach the centre of London was the Paddington Branch of the Grand Junction Canal which opened in July 1801. The Regent's Canal connected Paddington to the River Thames at Limehouse in 1820. The Paddington Canal was responsible for much of the industrial and social development of north west London. All these waterways were intensely busy in their commercial heyday, which lasted well into the second half of the twentieth century. There were some canals south of the river but these have all disappeared under urban development. There are many changes on the existing canals north of the river with huge developments at Paddington and Brentford.

51

Port-A-Bella Dock was once a council disposal point for domestic rubbish. The rubbish was taken by boats to fill holes left by quarrying around West Drayton on the outskirts of West London. In later years it became a restaurant and has been used as the headquarters of a prominent record company. Port-A-Bella Dock is at Ladbroke Grove close to the starting point for the Notting Hill Carnival that takes place annually at the end of August.

ABOVE Port-A-Bella Dock on the Paddington Canal at Ladbroke Grove.

The House Mill was built in 1776 and is the oldest and largest tidal mill in Britain. The Clock Mill was built later in 1817. Tidal mills work by allowing tidal water to flow upstream by holding ebbing water by the use of floodgates. The gates open when the downstream water level drops and the onrushing water turns the mill wheels.

All the Regent's Canal locks were duplicated because the canal was once so busy with commercial traffic. The locks in the picture below are actually known as Hampstead Road Locks and they are the only paired locks still in use.

LEFT Three Mills at Bow by the River Lee Navigation in East London has some of the finest waterside buildings in London.

BELOW Camden Lock, with its cosmopolitan market, is one of the best known places on London's canals. From here you can take a trip boat to Little Venice via London Zoo.

Brentford Transhipment Depot was busy up to the mid-1980s when most commercial water traffic had finally ended. Afterwards the warehouses remained active but goods were mostly moved by road transport. This picture was taken in 1965 when the depot was still thriving and bustling with barges and narrowboats.

RIGHT Most of the warehouses at Brentford Depot have gone and been replaced by housing, hotels and waterside bars.

The Canalway Cavalcade is an annual event during the first weekend of May at Little Venice. The water is packed with boats and the quayside has booths selling everything from food and books to plants for the garden. Little Venice is the starting place for passenger trip boats to London Zoo and Camden Lock. The island in the centre of the pool is named after the poet Robert Browning who lived in this area. It is possible that the name Little Venice originated with Browning who loved Venice where he died in 1889. From Little Venice it is a short walk to Paddington Waterside (formerly Paddington Basin) to see Europe's biggest modern waterside development.

ABOVE The Canalway Cavalcade at Little Venice.

RIGHT A pleasant afternoon taking tea on a waterside veranda above the Regent's Canal at Maida Hill near Little Venice.

Regent's Canal Dock, now known as Limehouse Basin, is shown above in May 1968. The vehicles lined up on the jetty are waiting to be loaded for export. The quaysides are busy with seagoing coasters and barges. The buildings in the background have all now disappeared as part of the Docklands development. The photograph was taken from a railway viaduct which was then disused, but is now part of the Docklands Light Railway.

RIGHT Limehouse Basin today has a large expanse of water devoted to moorings for a wide miscellany of canal and river craft. It is the home of the Cruising Association.

FAR RIGHT A small sailing boat passing Canary Wharf in London Docklands.

London's River

St Katharine Docks were once part of the London Docks. Now they have a new role as a yachting marina surrounded by hotels, shops and a pub. The docks attract many visitors because of their proximity to Tower Bridge and the Tower of London. The Queen's Rowbarge, *Gloriana* (seen to the right of the picture below) commemorated her Diamond Jubilee in 2012 and has a permanent mooring in the Docks. The building in the background is the Ivory House, one of the few original buildings that survived heavy wartime bombing.

RIGHT The Millennium Dome by the Thames on Greenwich Peninsula is now called the O2 Arena. It was an important venue during the London Olympic Games in 2012, staging gymnastics and basketball. It is now one of the world's busiest arenas, regularly hosting concerts and indoor sporting events.

A flotilla of boats leaves St Katharine Dock into the Pool of London by Tower Bridge. St Katharine Dock was built by Thomas Telford and was opened in 1828. The warehouses still remain and have been converted into apartments and shops. Thames sailing barges can often be seen in the dock. They were built for cargo carrying and continued to do so as late as the 1970s. Now they can be seen in full sail at regattas especially in the Thames estuary and at Maldon in Essex.

OPPOSITE The Queen Elizabeth II suspension bridge carries the southbound M25 motorway over the Thames at Dartford. It is the last crossing place across the river before the estuary. Northbound traffic has to go underground into tunnels. The bridge was opened in October 1991 and at busy times can carry 100,000 vehicles in a day.

This section of the Thames in Hammersmith is part of the annual Oxford and Cambridge Varsity Boat Race. In 1870 the original bridge at Hammersmith almost collapsed when 12,000 people crowded on it to watch the Boat Race. This bridge, built in 1827, was later demolished and the present structure designed by Sir Joseph Bazalgette was erected in 1887.

Sir Joseph Bazalgette (1819–1891) was the engineering genius who built the Thames Embankment in Central London following the cholera epidemic during the Big Stink of 1858. He also constructed London's first sewer network which was completed in 1866 and is still in use today.

RIGHT The tideway at Hammersmith in September 1980.

The Millennium footbridge across the Thames connects Bankside to St Paul's Cathedral. In the background is the Tate Modern art gallery and the Globe Theatre. There is now a continuous footpath on the south bank of the river between Westminster and Bermondsey.

ABOVE This view is from the top of St Paul's Cathedral.

LEFT Ice skating at Somerset House. Each year between mid-November and January, the grand courtyard at Somerset House is transformed into an ice rink.

Tower Bridge was designed by Sir Horace Jones and opened in 1894, seven years after his death. It was designed as a bascule bridge because of its proximity to the London docks when its central part would be lifted several times a day for passing ships. Although the docks have gone, the bridge is raised around 500 times a year for tall vessels. The high level walkway was the haunt of prostitutes and pickpockets and was closed in 1910.

The walkway has now been reopened to the public as part of the Tower Bridge Experience.

LEFT The Girl on a Dolphin statue is by David Wynne and was erected here in 1973.

Royal River

'Sweet Thames! Run softly, till I end my song.' EDMUND SPENSER

A new flood diversion channel known as the Jubilee River opened in June 2002 between Maidenhead and Windsor. January 2003 saw the worst floods on the river since 1947. The new channel came into use and avoided serious flooding at Maidenhead and Windsor. Some controversy arose when residents in the Wraysbury area complained that the new flood prevention scheme was actually increasing the flooding risk in their part of the river downstream.

ABOVE The Thames at Laleham during a period of winter flooding in January 1994.

ABOVE The thickly wooded Cliveden Reach on one of the finest sections of the River Thames.

RIGHT A tranquil part of the River Thames at Lower Shiplake. The village has literary connections with Alfred Lord Tennyson who married here in 1850 and George Orwell who lived here as a boy.

The present Cliveden House was built in 1851 on the site of an earlier one that burnt down. It was bought by the Astor family in 1893 and became a fashionable place for prominent figures in politics and the arts known as 'The Cliveden Set'. It was the location for a famous political scandal that nearly toppled the Government during the early 1960s. The house is now owned by the National Trust who lease it to a hotel group. Cliveden House has splendid gardens and woodland walks with wonderful views across the river from its lofty position.

Clifton Hampden Bridge has a medieval appearance although it was actually built in the Victorian Era. Jerome K Jerome wrote part of his classic Thames novel *Three Men in a Boat* while residing in the nearby Barley Mow Inn. The local church is perched on a rocky outcrop overlooking the river. In its churchyard is a memorial to Sergeant William Dykes who accidentally fired the first shot at the Battle of Waterloo and was subsequently courtmartialled by the Duke of Wellington.

Winter Hill near Marlow was a favourite place of Charles Dickens who loved to climb the hill and enjoy the extensive views over the Thames Valley. It is believed Kenneth Grahame used Winter Hill for the Wild Wood in his book *Wind in the Willows*.

LEFT Children play on a sand bar at the edge of the river while their grandparents enjoy the summer sunshine. This idyllic scene is by the Thames near Marlow.

A canal boat turns at the end of navigation on the Upper Thames at Inglesham. Behind the willow trees is the entrance to the long derelict Thames and Severn Canal. The first of several round houses typical to this canal can be seen by the first lock.

LEFT The infant River Thames near Kemble in Gloucestershire, only a mile from the river's source at Thames Head.

The River Avon at Offenham. Some of the locks on the River Avon were renamed after benefactors during the period of restoration. George Billington Lock is the first one on the Upper Avon and was built in the winter of 1969.

Shakespeare's Avon

The derelict southern section of the Stratford-upon-Avon Canal and the defunct Lower Avon Navigation were both restored and reopened in 1964. In each case voluntary labour was responsible for the successful campaign to reopen these beautiful waterways, against officialdom who in the main would have preferred to have left them closed. It took another ten years to complete the restoration of the Upper Avon which opened up the now popular Avon Cruising Ring. The highlight of the journey is, of course, Stratford-upon-Avon with its many Shakespearean connections.

BELOW The 17th century Eckington Bridge over the River Avon. There are glorious views as the river twists and winds around Bredon Hill in the Vale of Evesham.

Split bridges are one of the distinctive features of the Stratford-upon-Avon Canal. Two cast-iron cantilevered sections leave a gap that allows the boat horse's rope to pass through a fixed bridge without being unhitched.

BELOW Lapworth Locks on the southern Stratford-upon-Avon Canal. The beautiful scenery on this canal has made it one of the most popular waterways on the inland navigation system.

Bancroft Basin at Stratford-upon-Avon is where boats can stop to visit the town. The waterside is thronged with visitors from all over the world who take a special interest in watching boats pass through the lock between the basin and the River Avon. Shakespeare's birthplace, a 16th century half-timbered house with a beautiful cottage garden, is just a short walk from the canal. A Shakespeare memorial statue shows the bard looking over the canal basin surrounded by characters from his plays. The Royal Shakespeare Theatre is by the River Avon and the 15th century Clopton Bridge is now a footbridge over the river.

71

A branch canal from the Grand Union joins the Stratford-upon-Avon Canal at Kingswood Junction. This provides an alternative route into Birmingham from the south. During the years of decline on the canals the northern Stratford Canal was never shut down like its southern counterpart. Keeping the canal open became a cause célèbre when in 1947 the author Tom Rolt applied his right of navigation and forced the railway company to jack up a fixed bridge at Tunnel Lane, Kings Norton. The point was made with maximum press coverage and the action drew a large crowd who cheered Mr Rolt as he sailed past the obstacle.

A barrel-roofed lock cottage at Lowsonford on the southern Stratford-upon-Avon Canal. This is one of the few cottages of this type that remain unspoilt. Others have added extensions that are totally out of keeping with the original building. The reason for building the cottages in this way has never been properly explained. The theory that they were constructed by builders who only knew how to build bridges and tunnels is surely apocryphal.

Lowsonford is an attractive village that has a pub with a large waterside garden. The building of the Fleur de Lys pub was created from a former blacksmith's shop and a morgue. In later years the pub became famous for production of meat pies.

The Changing Face of Birmingham

LEFT The view from Old Turn Junction towards Broad Street in August 1973.

BELOW The same view from Old Turn Junction in 2005.

RIGHT A passenger trip boat at Old Turn Junction with the Barclaycard Arena in the background.

FAR RIGHT The trip boat *Jericho* waits for passengers outside the International Convention Centre.

BELOW RIGHT Brindley Place in Birmingham.

The part of Birmingham from Old Turn Junction towards Broad Street had become very run-down and most of the old factories were derelict. The picture shown above was taken in 1973 and within 20 years every building had gone including the church that stood above Broad Street Tunnel.

Compare the black and white picture with the colour photo (right) taken in 2005. The towpath bridges are all that remain. On the left of the colour picture is the International Convention Centre and a new pub. The National Sea Life Centre and Brindley Place are to the right. The Barclaycard Arena is behind the camera position. In the canal's commercial heyday, Old Turn Junction would have been congested with working boats resting up before heading to the Birmingham Main Line Canal, or to the Grand Junction Canal or the Worcester and Birmingham Canal.

The Barclaycard Arena, previously the National Indoor Arena, has become an important place to stage sporting and music events from tennis tournaments to the Eurovision Song Contest. It opened in 1991 and can seat 10,000 people. The International Convention Centre opened in 1991 and has seven halls including Symphony Hall, home of the City of Birmingham Symphony Orchestra.

Brindley Place has become a vibrant centre for Birmingham's nightlife with waterside restaurants and nightclubs. During the day, it is a popular place to spend an hour sitting at a café or bar watching the boats go past.

In 1975 Gas Street Basin still remained in its own private world, enclosed by warehouses and old canal buildings. At that time, the Hyatt Hotel and all today's modern buildings were a mere glint in the developer's eye.

RIGHT Birmingham's Gas Street Basin in October 1975.

BELOW Boats in Gas Street Basin dominated by the Hyatt Hotel's glass monolith.

'The Back of the Map'

'The Back of the Map' was a term used by the working boatmen to describe the Dudley and Stourbridge canals. These highly industrialised waterways connected the Staffs and Worcester Canal to the rest of the Black Country canals. Three long tunnels were required to pierce the Rowley Hills; Netherton Tunnel is the only one still in regular use by motorboats. Dudley Tunnel, although restored, is only used by electrically powered craft from the nearby Black Country Living Museum. This is because of inadequate ventilation inside the tunnel. Lapal Tunnel that once connected the Dudley Canal to the Worcester and Birmingham Canal was never stable and eventually the roof collapsed forcing the tunnel to close in 1917.

BELOW Stourbridge Locks with the Redhouse Glassworks Cone. This part of Stourbridge is known as the Glass Quarter and the Cone now houses a museum celebrating the work of the Stuart Crystal Glassworks.

Delph Locks at Brierley Hill carry the Dudley Canal down to a junction with the Stourbridge Canal at the bottom of the hill. When this picture was taken in August 1973, there was a coal mine with its attendant slag heaps at the bottom of the flight.

BELOW Compare the black and white picture with the colour photo taken 25 years later. The colliery has gone and been replaced by a housing estate.

Windmill End Junction on the Dudley Canal is a watery crossroads spanned by a series of delightful and elegant cast iron bridges. They were cast at Horseley Iron Works in the Black Country. The ruins of Cobb's Engine House stands close by the entrance to Netherton Tunnel. Built around 1830, it once pumped water from one of the many mines dotted around these hillsides. It remains as a stark emblem of the region's industrial past. Now the Rowley Hills provide a welcome touch of greenery in an intensely built-up area.

The Black Country Living Museum at Dudley describes itself as having '26 acres of Living History to Explore'. It includes a Black Country village built around an old canal arm and the approach to Dudley Tunnel. One of the main visitor attractions is an underground voyage by electric boat into the caverns of the Dudley Tunnel. The bridge in the photos below was moved here from its original place over the canal in Wolverhampton.

TOP RIGHT A village street at the Black Country Living Museum leading down to the Boat Dock.

BELOW The museum under construction in 1976. In the picture contractors are securing the bridge in its present position.

RIGHT The same bridge in its permanent place at the entrance to the village.

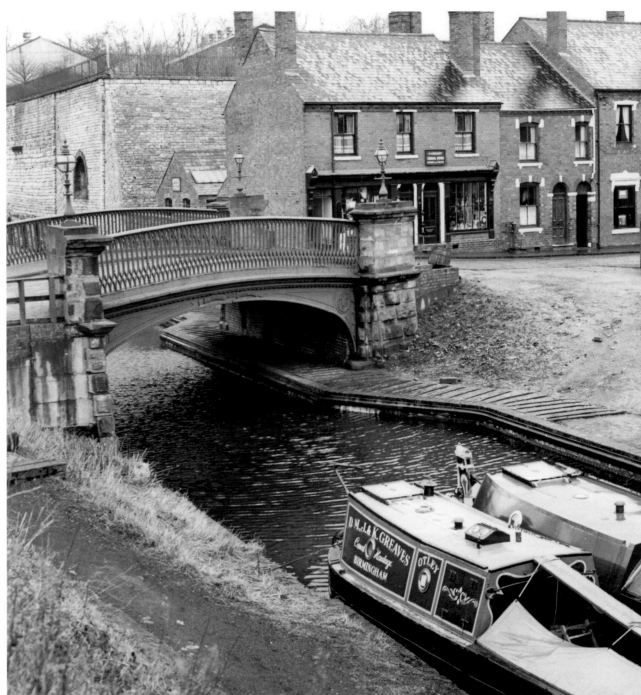

Canals in Manchester

The Manchester Ship Canal was opened in 1894 and was the last major canal built in Britain. It runs for 36 miles from the tidal River Mersey at Eastham to Manchester. Manchester Docks at the head of the ship canal closed to commercial traffic in the early 1980s. It was redeveloped for housing, commerce and recreation and renamed Salford Quays. Present day attractions include the Imperial War Museum North and the Lowry Centre with its art gallery, theatre and restaurants. The Lowry Centre contains 300 paintings by the Manchester-born artist who specialised in painting the local industrial scene with its 'matchstick men and matchstick cats and dogs'.

BELOW The Victoria Building at Salford Quays looks like Manchester's answer to the Taj Mahal.

The bridge at Dukinfield Junction is the meeting place of three canals – the Ashton Canal from central Manchester, the Peak Forest Canal from Whaley Bridge and the Huddersfield Narrow Canal. The Portland Basin Industrial Museum is opposite the bridge where there is also a collection of vintage canal boats. The original warehouse was derelict for years following a disastrous fire in the 1970s. It was restored in 1999 as the Portland Basin Museum which houses industrial and community-based exhibits.

RIGHT The bridge at Dukinfield Junction at Ashton-under-Lyne in eastern Manchester.

Castle Quay is where the Duke of Bridgewater's Canal ended its journey from the Duke's mines at Worsley. There are some splendid restored warehouses in this area which have been converted to new uses. In recent years, Castlefield has become Manchester's trendy centre for pubs, restaurants and nightclubs.

ABOVE Castle Quay at Castlefield in the centre of Manchester.

ABOVE Albion Mills Lock on the Deansgate Flight, popularly known as the Rochdale Nine. These locks are part of the Rochdale Canal which at one end has a junction with the Ashton Canal at Ancoats and meets the Bridgewater Canal at the other. This last section of the Rochdale Canal is flanked by nightclubs, discos and restaurants.

RIGHT Ancoats Locks in Manchester.

OPPOSITE The Peak Forest Canal clings to the hillside above the River Goyt valley to the south east of Manchester. This section is at Strines which is between Marple and Whaley Bridge.

The Ashton Canal in eastern Manchester is a short urban canal, which has 18 locks in just over 6 miles. The main highlight of the journey is the City of Manchester Stadium by Beswick Locks where the 2002 Commonwealth Games were held. It is now the home of Manchester City Football Club. The Ashton Canal lay derelict and rubbish-filled for many years before being reopened in 1974. Although it is unlikely to win any prizes for its scenic beauty, it is nevertheless an integral part of the Cheshire Cruising Ring.

Cargoes on the Peak Forest Canal once crossed the hills of the Peak District from Whaley Bridge to the Cromford Canal by means of the Cromford and High Peak Railway. Buxworth Basin was an important interchange point where tramways connected the canal with the Doveholes limestone quarries. After years of disuse, the basin is again navigable by boat and its limekilns have been restored.

Canals in Wales

This photograph shows walkers on the wooded Monmouthshire and Brecon Canal near Llangynidr. Affectionately known as the 'Mon and Brec', this beautiful, isolated canal lies mostly within the Brecon Beacons National Park. This picture was taken in June 1972 shortly after the canal had been reopened for navigation.

Until recently Pontymoile Basin, two miles south of Mamhilad, was the southern limit of navigation on this canal. Now restorers have extended the navigation three miles towards Cwmbran. In time it is hoped to reach Newport which is 5 miles and 30 locks away.

RIGHT The Monmouthshire and Brecon Canal at Mamhilad near Pontypool.

Llanfoist was the site of a tramroad over the Blorenge mountain where trucks brought their loads from limestone quarries. A second line linked the ironworks at Blaenavon with the canal wharf. It is hard to believe that this enchanted spot on the Monmouthshire and Brecon Canal was once a place of intense industrial activity.

ABOVE The building to the right of the picture was once a warehouse with a loading wharf from the tramroad to the canal.

OPPOSITE A misty autumn morning in Llangollen.

The Llangollen Canal is one of Britain's most popular cruising waterways. Towering above the town of Llangollen are the ancient ruins of Castell Dinas Bran. The castle was built around 1260 and occupies the site of a former Iron Age hillfort. The poet William Wordsworth visited the ruin and afterwards wrote 'Relics of Kings, wreck of forgotten wars, to the winds abandoned and the prying stars'.

LEFT Sun Trevor Bridge near Llangollen, with its canalside pub, is a favourite stopping place for boaters. The mountain in the background has the remains of Castell Dinas Bran and overlooks the town of Llangollen.

The bridge shown in the picture below is on the final narrow section of the Llangollen Canal before reaching the end of the navigation at the Horseshoe Falls. It was originally built as a feeder, bringing water from the River Dee to the canal, and later made navigable. Llangollen is the home of the International Musical Eisteddfod that attracts performers and visitors from all over the world each July. It also has a steam railway that runs for eight miles beside the River Dee.

LEFT The disused Neath Canal near Swansea in South Wales is slowly being restored in short sections. A new aqueduct has been built and three locks have recently been restored. There are now two restored lengths along the beautiful Vale of Neath. The picture shows the trip boat *Thomas Dadford* on a section near Resolven.

LEFT The Montgomery Canal connects to the Llangollen Canal at Welsh Frankton near Ellesmere. Boats moved limestone from the quarries along the route but otherwise it was a mainly agricultural waterway. Never profitable, it fell into disuse and became derelict. Six miles at the top of the canal have now been reopened along with a 12-mile section around Welshpool in the middle. That leaves an awkward eight-mile derelict section before the two halves can be reunited. The picture shows the canal at Buttington Wharf near Welshpool.

Canals in Scotland

Opened in 1822, the Caledonian Canal follows the geological fault line of the Great Glen and makes it possible for seagoing boats to avoid the hazardous journey around Scotland's northern coast. The construction was a huge undertaking and provided work for thousands of Highlanders during a period of high unemployment. Built by Thomas Telford and considered by many as his masterpiece, the 60-mile-long waterway has 22 miles of artificial canal linking 38 miles of natural lochs.

ABOVE View of the Caledonian Canal at Laggan Bridge.

Laggan Cut was the biggest obstacle in building the Caledonian Canal. Hundreds of workmen (known as navvies) spent over seven years digging out the channel with picks and shovels which was all that was available to them at that time. It all looks very natural now, but then it would have been a blot on the landscape similar to today's motorway construction.

ABOVE Caledonian Canal at Laggan Cut.

RIGHT A pleasure craft leaves Laggan Locks and heads out into Loch Lochy.

ABOVE Urquhart Castle on the shore of Loch Ness, which is part of the Caledonian Canal.

RIGHT A fishing boat shares a lock with pleasure cruisers at Banavie Locks near Fort William.

The village of Drumnadrochit is the tourist centre for the legendary Loch Ness Monster. The first modern sighting of the monster was in 1933 which sparked off much interest and speculation. A Loch Ness Investigation Bureau was set up in the 1960s to investigate the phenomenon. Cameras were set up with underwater listening devices and sonar scanners, but no evidence of a monster was found. The myth of the Loch Ness Monster attracts thousands of visitors each year and has spawned a thriving 'Nessie' industry in that part of the Highlands.

This magnificent flight of eight locks at Banavie is popularly known as 'Neptune's Staircase'. There are more staircase locks at Inverness and Fort Augustus. Staircase locks are more economical to build than conventional lock flights which have a waiting section between each chamber. In practice they can become bottlenecks for boating traffic as passage through them is very slow. (See Bingley Five Rise Locks on page 34.)

Built in 1809, the Crinan Canal cuts across the Kintyre Peninsula, avoiding a difficult 130-mile journey around the Mull of Kintyre. The canal is 9 miles long with 15 locks and runs from Ardrishaig to Crinan Harbour. The Clyde Puffers regularly used the canal as a safe route between Glasgow and Inverness. The sailors on the Puffers sang a song whose chorus sums up why they used the Crinan Canal:

'Oh! The Crinan Canal for me,
I don't like the wild raging sea,
The big foaming breakers would give me the shakers,
The Crinan Canal for me.'

ABOVE Crinan Canal at Cairnbaan.

RIGHT Cairnbaan has four locks and is about half way along the Crinan Canal.

94

The construction of the Forth and Clyde Canal allowed seagoing coasters to reach Glasgow and to navigate across the middle of Scotland. It was very busy in its early days until railway competition and the closure of Grangemouth Docks to merchant shipping during World War I took away much of its regular traffic. In 1962 the canal was closed when the new A80 road forced the canal into a culvert at Castlecary. It stayed closed until 2001 when the waterway was reopened and reconnected to the Union Canal by the amazing Falkirk Wheel (see page 157).

ABOVE Auchinstarry is regarded as one of the most scenic stretches on the 35-mile-long canal.

The 32-mile-long Union Canal connects Edinburgh to the Forth and Clyde Canal via the Falkirk Wheel. It has no locks, and so remains on a level contour throughout its length. To achieve this preservation of water, a number of impressive aqueducts and one tunnel were constructed.

RIGHT The Almond Aqueduct is near Ratho on the outskirts of Edinburgh.

BELOW Leamington Lift Bridge is near the Union Canal terminus in the centre of Edinburgh. From here it is only a short walk to Princes Street and Edinburgh Castle.

Old Kilpatrick is reputed to be the birthplace of St Patrick who was driven to Ireland by the Devil who threw rocks at him. One of the rocks landed in the middle of the River Clyde so a navigation light was placed upon it and called St Patrick's Stone Light. The Erskine Bridge towers above the canal at Old Kilpatrick before crossing the River Clyde. It was opened in 1971 and provides an alternative route between the Highlands and the south by avoiding central Glasgow.

LEFT The Forth and Clyde Canal between Bowling and Old Kilpatrick.

BELOW Bowling Basin is the terminus for the Forth and Clyde Canal at the western edge of Glasgow. Two sea locks give access into the wide River Clyde. The basin is now used for pleasure craft mooring.

East Anglian Waterways

A typical Broads scene has sailing boat, motor cruiser and windmill. This is at How Hill on the River Ant where there is a 365 acre study centre. The estate has reed beds, marsh, woodland and a lake together with three restored drainage mills and a marshman's cottage. The study centre is owned by the How Hill Trust who run residential field courses for children and young people. The River Ant is narrower than the other Broads rivers and is navigable for eight miles.

The Broads of Norfolk and Suffolk are a complex series of shallow lakes linked by navigable rivers. It is a flat landscape of marshes and reed beds providing habitats for a wide variety of wildlife. It is also the most popular boating area in Britain. The Broads were formed because of medieval peat diggings for use as fuel. The holes left behind filled up when water levels rose.

In 1978, the Broads Authority was formed to look after the region, and in 1989 it was given the status of a National Park. The sailing boat in the picture is near Acle Bridge on the River Bure. Acle Bridge was once a favourite place for executing criminals. Local folklore claims to have seen ghosts dangling over the parapet of the bridge.

ABOVE River Ant at How Hill.

TOP RIGHT Sailing on the River Bure at Acle Bridge.

RIGHT The Norfolk Wherry was the traditional Norfolk Broads sailing boat originally used for trading. *Albion*, one of the last surviving wherries, is now available for hire, and on this occasion was out on a school cruise on the River Ant.

ABOVE Although it is open to navigation, the 20-mile-long New Bedford River is tidal and was built as a flood relief channel. Most boats take the more interesting route along the Old River Ouse past Ely.

LEFT This chapel bridge at St Ives was built in 1414, replacing a previous wooden structure.

RIGHT Ely Cathedral and the River Great Ouse.

St Ives Bridge on the River Great Ouse is a 15th century chantry chapel bridge. Chapels were built on bridges for the spiritual needs of travellers who could give thanks after a long and arduous journey. They were called chantry chapels because masses were sung for the wellbeing of travellers and for the souls of victims of highway violence. They were common in the Middle Ages but most of them have disappeared over the years, leaving just four examples. They can be found at Wakefield, Rotherham, Bradford-on-Avon and at St Ives.

The octagonal lantern tower of Ely Cathedral makes it visible for miles across the flat landscape of the Fens. Originally a Saxon church, it became a cathedral in 1109 at the time of William the Conqueror. It was built from limestone quarried at Barnack near Stamford in Lincolnshire, and is one of the finest examples of Romanesque architecture. Oliver Cromwell closed it for ten years and used it as stables for his cavalry horses. The cathedral is noted for its stained glass windows and contains a Stained Glass Museum. The Priors Door is an excellent example of Norman craftsmanship.

Stretham Old Engine was built in 1831 and was one of many steam powered drainage engines in the Fens. It pumped water from reclaimed land that was below sea level. The steam engine worked until 1941 when it was replaced by diesel power. The old engine has been preserved along with its tools in the pumping house which is open for public viewing. Stretham Old Engine is by the River Great Ouse a few miles south of Ely.

ABOVE Springtime by the Old River Nene.

The twin Fenland villages of Upwell and Outwell sit on the daffodil-clad banks of the old course of the River Nene. Hereward the Wake lived here for a while after his defeat by the Normans. Originally called Welle, it was then the longest village in Britain. The villages assumed their present names when they were split.

Western Canals

The restoration of the derelict Thames and Severn Canal and Stroudwater Navigation is a massive task. Altogether there are 36 miles of waterway comprising 57 locks and a long leaky tunnel at Sapperton. The Thames and Severn, beset with water supply problems, finally closed in 1933. The Stroudwater Navigation lasted for another 21 years, before it too capitulated. Now reunited as the Cotswold Canals, it is just a question of how long and how much it will cost to restore these astonishingly beautiful waterways. The Cotswold Canal Trust, with nearly 8,000 members in 2015, was formed to promote the reopening of the canals.

Over 70 years have passed since this section of the Thames and Severn Canal at Stantons Bridge near Stroud last saw a boat passing through. Although restoration is well under way, there are many locks to be rebuilt. Another major restoration problem is returning the navigation to Brimscombe Port where the canal has been built over for offices and car parks.

RIGHT A misty morning on the Thames and Severn Canal at Thrupp near Stroud.

BELOW The Round House at Chalford on the Thames and Severn Canal. These conical roofed lock cottages are only found on this waterway and no-one knows why they were built this way. Five of them have survived on the Thames and Severn.

Gloucester Docks has become a popular centre for visitors. It is hard to believe that the superb old warehouses were once threatened with demolition because they were in such poor condition. Now one of them houses the National Waterways Museum and others have been converted to a variety of uses.

Built as a ship canal, the Gloucester and Sharpness Canal is 16 miles long between Gloucester Docks and the River Severn at Sharpness Docks. It features distinctive bridge-keepers' cottages fronted with Doric porticoes and passes close to the Wildfowl Centre at Slimbridge.

ABOVE Gloucester Docks.

LEFT The Gloucester and Sharpness Canal at Frampton-on-Severn in Gloucestershire.

The 50-mile-long Wilts and Berks Canal has been derelict for over a hundred years and many of its urban sections have been built over. Despite this the Wilts and Berks Canal Trust are gaining support for its eventual return to navigation and work parties are regularly engaged on restoration.

Lord Rolle built his six-mile canal between Torrington and Bideford in 1823. The most impressive feature was this five-arched aqueduct. The canal has long gone but the aqueduct remains in good condition. It supports the driveway to Beam House which once belonged to the Rolle family and is now an adventure holiday centre. Henry Williamson's famous book *Tarka the Otter* was set on the River Torridge at Beam. In the book the aqueduct is referred to as the Canal Bridge.

LEFT The Wilts and Berks Canal at Dauntsey.

ABOVE Lord Rolle's Aqueduct is a five-arched aqueduct over the River Torridge in North Devon.

Southern Waterways

Pulteney Bridge over the River Avon in Bath was designed by Robert Adam and built in 1769. It is built in the Palladian style and is one of the few remaining shop-lined bridges in the world. Bath is a prominent city on the tourist trail with its Roman Baths, Abbey and the Royal Crescent. The Kennet and Avon Canal passes through Sydney Gardens before losing its canal status at the River Avon at the foot of Bath Locks.

ABOVE Pulteney Bridge.

RIGHT Cleveland House in Sydney Gardens was once the headquarters of the Kennet and Avon Canal Company.

The ten-mile section between Bradford-on-Avon and Bath contains two major aqueducts over the Avon valley and some of the most dramatic scenery found anywhere on the British canals. The nearby pumping station at Claverton was built in 1810 and could pump 100,000 gallons of water from the River Avon into the canal, 47 feet above the river. A giant waterwheel that provided the power has been restored, but the task has now been taken over by electrically controlled pumps.

BELOW Mooring outside the George Inn at Bathampton on the Kennet and Avon Canal.

Caen Hill Locks provide the best example to canal restorers that nothing is impossible. This formidable flight of locks was once totally derelict but is now back to full navigation. The Kennet and Avon was reopened in 1990 and connects the Thames at Reading to the Avon at Bath. It is 93 miles long and has 104 locks.

ABOVE Caen Hill Locks at Devizes on the Kennet and Avon Canal.

RIGHT This lovely place on the River Wey is about as far south as you can travel by boat on the connected inland waterway system.

The River Wey was one of the earliest river navigations in Britain. It opened from the Thames at Weybridge and ran to Guildford in 1653. It was extended to Godalming as the Godalming Navigation 80 years later. The waterway was privately owned for many years until 1964 when it was presented to the National Trust. Guildford is the only built-up part of the 20-mile navigation which mostly passes through beautiful Surrey countryside. It has junctions with the Basingstoke Canal and the disused Wey and Arun Canal.

ABOVE Aylesford on the River Medway.

Aylesford is on the tidal section of the River Medway. This beautiful river is one of the far flung outposts on the inland waterway system as it requires a potentially hazardous journey around the Thames estuary to reach it. Once into this delightful river there are over 40 miles of cruising waterway through the Garden of England. Tradition states that the river separates The Men of Kent from the Kentish Men. The Men of Kent are born on the eastern side of the river while the Kentish Men come from the west. The division originates from when the Jutes partitioned Kent into two areas over 1,500 years ago. In 1066 it is said that the Men of Kent resisted the invading William the Conqueror with more verve than the Kentish Men who surrendered.

Towpath walking is generally on flat ground and so is very popular with people who are not into hill trekking. The seven miles between Crookham Wharf and Odiham Castle offer one of the finest stretches for boating or towpath walking in the country. The Basingstoke Canal reopened in 1991 following a massive rebuilding campaign by volunteers and two county councils. It is probably one of the most wooded canals, which is surprising as the first part between the River Wey and Fleet passes through a densely populated region.

ABOVE Walkers enjoy the Basingstoke Canal near Winchfield.

PART TWO

LEFT A train of 'Tom Puddings' approaching Pollington Lock on the Aire and Calder Navigation in 1968.

King Coal

Coal was the most important commodity carried on Britain's inland waterways. Over the years the Yorkshire waterways have carried vast quantities of coal to fuel Britain's industry and also for export. The Aire and Calder Navigation is still a commercial waterway but most of the collieries have closed down and coal carrying is now just a memory.

'Tom Puddings' were invented around 1860 and were floating containers, each capable of carrying 40 tons of coal. In 1913 there were over a thousand 'Tom Puddings' working on the Yorkshire waterways. They were discontinued in 1986. An example can be seen as an exhibit at the Yorkshire Waterway Museum at Goole Docks.

RIGHT A coal compartment on the Aire and Calder Navigation at Castleford in July 1968 when coal was still the most important cargo carried on the waterway.

BELOW The same position in 2003 with a loaded sand and gravel barge.

The Ferrybridge 'C' power station on the Aire and Calder Navigation no longer operates on fossil fuel so coal is not required any more. Most of the former loading wharves have since been planted with trees and landscaped. In November 1965 three cooling towers collapsed in a high wind and were completely destroyed.

ABOVE A busy scene at Ferrybridge 'C' power station in July 1982. Coal barges wait to be unloaded at the wharf while an empty coal barge passes an oil tanker.

'Tom Puddings' were taken to Goole Docks and then each container was lifted from the water and tipped into the ship's hold. This was the last of five working hoists in Goole Docks and it has been preserved as an exhibit for the Yorkshire Waterway Museum. The museum tells the story of the Port of Goole, the transportation of coal and the lives of barge and boating families. The town and port owes its very existence to the arrival of the Aire and Calder Navigation in 1826. Before then Goole was a mere village nestling in the marshes beside the River Ouse.

ABOVE The Goole Boat Hoist emptying coal from 'Tom Puddings' into a collier ship in May 1974.

Cut and Fill

Gnosall is a favourite stopping place for visiting boaters on the Shropshire Union Canal. Shelmore Embankment about a mile and a half north of Gnosall was one of the major achievements in building the canal. Constant collapsing of the embankment meant that Shelmore was the last obstacle in completing the waterway, which eventually opened in 1835.

BELOW Shropshire Union Canal at Gnosall.

RIGHT Cowley Cutting on the Shropshire Union Canal ends with a tunnel before entering Gnosall village. This is one of several deep cuttings on this canal. Although canal building techniques were much improved since Brindley's day, digging precipitous gorges like this was still done by pick, shovel and wheelbarrows.

The Birmingham and Liverpool Junction Canal was one of the last canals to be built in Britain. Engineered by Thomas Telford and completed in 1835, it ignored the contoured ramblings of its predecessors by hardly deviating from a straight line. Telford's 'cut and fill' technique built deep cuttings and high embankments. When locks were needed they were built in flights. The Birmingham and Liverpool connected the Staffs and Worcester Canal at Wolverhampton to the old Chester Canal at Nantwich. The Chester Canal was built much earlier between Nantwich and Ellesmere Port. In later years the two canals combined as the Shropshire Union Canal.

The Boat Museum at Ellesmere Port is where the Shropshire Union Canal meets the Manchester Ship Canal. It spreads over seven acres of this former transhipment port. It has the world's largest floating collection of canal craft with eight indoor exhibitions inside historic buildings. The museum also has a working forge, craft workshops and a row of cottages representing different decades of the Victorian era.

Further south at Market Drayton, five locks drop the canal through a beautiful sandstone cutting. The cavernous Woodseaves Cutting can be found just south of Tyrley Top Lock. Market Drayton was the birthplace of Robert Clive who became known as Clive of India (1725–1774). As a young man in the 1750s he fought the French in India, eventually clearing the way for British rule for the next hundred years. Market Drayton is also renowned for its cheese and gingerbread.

ABOVE The Boat Museum at Ellesmere Port.

RIGHT The Shropshire Union Canal at Tyrley Locks near Market Drayton.

The Boat Horse

Before the advent of powered boats, it was horsepower that moved the canal boats. The horse became one of the family and it was often the job of the boatman's children to lead the horse along the towpath. Many tunnels had no towpath so the horse had to be led over the top while the boatman 'legged' his craft underground.

Boat horses required stabling at night and stables were provided at wharves and canalside pubs. Blacksmiths were needed to replace worn out shoes and corn needed to be available to feed the horses. Many of the older generation of boatmen didn't like what they called 'them new-fangled motors' and carried on working with horses well into the 20th century.

ABOVE A legacy of the days of horse boating can be seen in many places on the canals with grooving on bridge plates like this one on the Shropshire Union Canal. Constant rubbing by taut wet tow ropes has eaten into the cast iron plate put there to protect the brick or stonework of the bridge.

LEFT The last working boat horse on the Black Country Canals at Smethwick Locks in December 1970. This boat carried rubbish on the Birmingham Canal. Experienced horses working along a familiar route would remember where to stop or slow down without anyone having to lead them. A working horse like this one would know when to stop at the approach to a lock..

OPPOSITE 'Bonnie' the boat horse pulling boat *Maria* near Ivinghoe on the Grand Union Canal. They were travelling from Manchester to London for a boat rally in July 2000.

In general boat horses were hard worked but well looked after. There were exceptions as noted by Arnold Bennett in July 1873 – almost exactly a hundred years earlier than this photograph. He described a scene on the Trent and Mersey Canal in the Potteries where 'an unhappy skeleton of a horse floundered in a towpath quagmire being whipped by a seven-year old girl around its crooked large jointed legs'.

Horse-drawn boats can still be seen at various places on the inland waterways pulling public trip boats.

ABOVE Horse-drawn boat *Hyades* on the Grand Union Canal at Fenny Stratford, Bletchley in June 1973. Young enthusiasts were trying to revive the art of commercial trading using a boat horse in the traditional manner.

ABOVE This horse-drawn boat was on the Ashby Canal near the Bosworth Battlefield site. Unfortunately the service has been discontinued.

LEFT The Kennet Valley horse-drawn trip boat operates from Kintbury on the Kennet and Avon Canal. It is available for hire between April and October and can accommodate 70 passengers.

Steam Boats

With steam belching out from every orifice, the splendid steam dredger *Perseverance* is seen here working on the Basingstoke Canal in October 1980. This 70-ton pontoon dredger worked for 15 years digging out sludge and silt from the western part of the Basingstoke Canal. The Canal was eventually reopened in 1991. The dredger is now an exhibit in the Boat Museum at Ellesmere Port.

ABOVE After twenty years rotting away in a Thames backwater, steam driven narrowboat *Tixall* has been restored and was seen here at Napton on the Oxford Canal on its way to a new home in August 2005.

OPPOSITE Steam Puffer *VIC 32* leaving Laggan Locks on the Caledonian Canal in the Scottish Highlands.

The VIC series of Clyde Puffers was built to service warships during World War II. VIC is an acronym for Victualler Inshore Craft. Built in 1939, *VIC 32* carried ammunition and fuel during the war. Since 1975 it has been used as a pleasure boat taking steam enthusiasts on cruises around the Western Isles and the Crinan and Caledonian Canals.

President was built in 1909 by the famous canal carrying company Fellows Morton and Clayton. They built 31 similar craft between 1889 and 1931. Although they were very powerful, steam narrowboats could only carry 12 tons compared with 25 by a horse-drawn boat. The boat is now owned by the Black Country Living Museum.

ABOVE AND RIGHT Steam driven narrowboat *President* at Wolverhampton Locks.

Restoration

The *Zachariah Keppel* is named after the contractor responsible for building most of the original Wey and Arun Canal. The Drungewick Aqueduct is used by the Wey and Arun Canal Trust Boat for passenger trips on the restored section at Loxwood.

ABOVE Trip boat *Zachariah Keppel* in the new lock at Loxwood.

LEFT The new Drungewick Aqueduct opened in 2003.

Graham Palmer was the founder and inspiration of the Waterway Recovery Group. Sometimes called 'The Dirty Weekenders', these hard working volunteers have been at the heart of every successful restoration project since 1970. The store hut and WC is named Melbury House, which was an irreverent joke aimed at the headquarters of the British Waterways Board. Graham Palmer died in 1988 at the early age of 48.

ABOVE Graham Palmer, complete with trademark woolly hat, at the Stratford-upon-Avon Canal in April 1976.

RIGHT Waterway Recovery Group volunteers working at Wilmcote Locks on the Stratford-upon-Avon Canal in 1976.

BELOW A new lock on the northern section of the Montgomery Canal was named Graham Palmer Lock. There is a plaque to the memory of the founder of the Waterway Recovery Group – complete with woolly hat!

The present lock-free Ashby Canal ends at Snarestone, but an isolated section at Moira has been restored. It was necessary to construct a new lock in order to continue the canal northwards. A new section of canal will have to be built around the town of Measham before the two separate parts of the Ashby Canal can be completed.

ABOVE Digging a new channel at Moira at the top of the Ashby Canal in July 2001.

RIGHT One of the major restoration stories in recent years was the successful return to navigation of the Kennet and Avon Canal. Widmead Lock near Newbury was one of the last locks to be completed. This picture shows work in progress at Widmead Lock in March 1990.

ABOVE LTC Rolt wrote a book *Narrow Boat* about his travels around the decaying canal system in 1939 on board his boat *Cressy*. This plaque at Tom Rolt Bridge in Banbury is but a few yards from Tooley's Boatyard where his voyage began. Tom Rolt, Robert Aickman and waterway historian Charles Hadfield formed the Inland Waterways Association in 1946. The IWA campaigned to increase national awareness of canals and their future in leisure and commerce. Without their efforts, officialdom would have allowed most of the remaining canals to run down towards final abandonment.

ABOVE This plaque at Tardebigge Top Lock on the Worcester and Birmingham Canal commemorates the famous meeting in 1946 between Robert Aickman and Tom and Angela Rolt that led to the founding of the Inland Waterways Association.

RIGHT Volunteers restoring a lock at Hanbury on the Droitwich Canal. The restored Droitwich Canals provide a picturesque short cut between the Worcester and Birmingham Canal and the River Severn.

Painted Boats

A working narrowboat was 70 feet long and 7 feet wide. The boatman's cabin was 8 to 9 feet long and less than 7 feet wide, and this tiny cabin was home to the boatman and his family. It was a life of hard work, low pay and dirty cargoes like coal, so it is not surprising that the boat people felt the need to brighten their lives by painting their home in bright colours. They painted bold designs in contrasting colours and developed the traditional 'Roses and Castle' theme which is an art form exclusive to canal boats.

BELOW Wooden tank narrowboat *Gifford* at Braunston on the Grand Union Canal. These unpowered butty boats were built by Thomas Clayton to carry bulk liquids like tar and crude oil. *Gifford* is now owned by the Boat Museum Society.

ABOVE A fanciful scene on a boat cabin depicting a medieval castle with a canal bridge in the foreground.

RIGHT A waterway artist painting a water can outside the Canal Museum at Stoke Bruerne on the Grand Union Canal.

A boatman often painted his name on the water can so it was easily identified in case of theft from its place on the cabin roof. A water can had several domestic uses, from peeling potatoes to washing the boatman's socks. A second can was used purely for drinking water.

Hotel boats are usually very colourful and well presented by their owners. Hotel boating is an ideal holiday for people who don't want the trouble of handling a boat or working locks. You can enjoy a holiday just looking at the passing scenery, reading a book and waiting to be fed.

ABOVE A pair of hotel boats at Braunston on the Grand Union Canal.

LEFT A colourful privately owned boat on the Trent and Mersey Canal. Note the painted tiller, the cabin doors, and a glimpse of brasswork in the cabin's interior.

The Anderton Lift

The Anderton Lift was designed by Edward Leader Williams, who was later responsible for building the Manchester Ship Canal. Electricity replaced steam in 1903 and counterbalanced weights replaced the hydraulic system in 1908. In more recent times the lift suffered severe corrosion because of chemical pollution from nearby works and in 1983 it had to be closed for safety reasons. Restored and reopened in 2002, it has a visitor centre with displays and information about its history, and a trip boat, which gives visitors the opportunity of experiencing the lift at first hand. The Anderton Lift has now become one of the most popular tourist attractions in north-west England.

LEFT The Anderton Lift and adjacent depot with a coaster in May 1968. The depot is now a freight terminal for road vehicles and the wharf is only used for storage.

LEFT A section of the iron gearing on top of the Anderton Lift.

RIGHT The boat in the foreground is the 100-year-old *Saturn* that was once a horse-drawn fly-boat carrying perishable goods non-stop day and night. In more recent years *Saturn* carried the runner bearing the Olympic torch over the Pontcysyllte Aqueduct on the Llangollen Canal.

Aqueducts

The North Circular Aqueduct was built in 1933 when the North Circular Road was constructed. It was replaced by a bigger one 60 years later when the road was widened. Removing the old aqueduct and getting the new one into place without interrupting traffic on one of London's busiest roads, proved to be a masterpiece of ingenuity.

RIGHT The new North Circular Aqueduct is considerably wider than the original and has two channels for the boats. It is the only large structure on the lock-free Paddington Canal that runs from Bulls Bridge, Southall, to Little Venice.

BELOW A pair of narrowboats cross the North Circular Aqueduct in London in August 1980.

ABOVE Marple Aqueduct on the Lower Peak Forest Canal near Stockport.

The Marple Aqueduct was built in 1800 and took seven years to complete. Seven men were killed during its construction. The aqueduct spans the deep, wooded gorge of the River Goyt, and the holes in the stone abutments are to relieve pressure on the arches. This picture was taken in May 1974 shortly after the canal had been reopened following years of neglect. The Lower Peak Forest Canal is now part of the popular Cheshire Ring cruising circuit.

The English author George Borrow saw Marple Aqueduct and wrote 'Few things so beautiful in their origins as this canal, which it be known, with its locks and aqueducts, the grandest of which is the stupendous erection near Stockport'.

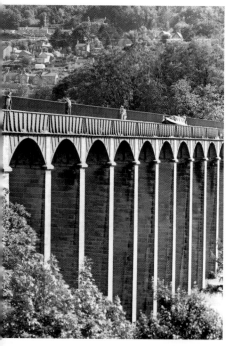

ABOVE AND RIGHT The Pontcysyllte Aqueduct, now a World Heritage Site.

Pontcysyllte is the longest, highest and most famous of Britain's aqueducts. 1007 feet in length and 126 feet high, it carries the Llangollen Canal across the Valley of the River Dee. It was designed by Thomas Telford and William Jessop and was completed in 1805. Boats travel in a cast iron trough which has a suspended towpath on one side but nothing but space on the other. It leaves the boat's helmsman with a vertigo-inducing view of the valley below.

The engineer John Rennie built several aqueducts on the Lancaster and Kennet and Avon Canals. Dundas aqueduct near Bath on the Kennet and Avon is one of his finest. It was built in golden Bath stone which proved to be unsuitable for long lasting wear. Rennie wanted to build in brick but the canal company overruled him. It was opened in 1800 but required treatment for frost damage within three years. Despite structural patching over the years, Dundas Aqueduct, with its balustrades and cornices, remains one of Rennie's masterpieces. It was named after Charles Dundas who was the original chairman of the Kennet and Avon Canal Company and in 1951 became the first canal structure to be scheduled as an ancient monument.

Waterside Inns

There are many famous and historic inns on the river at Henley but few have a more advantageous position than The Angel on the Bridge. You will need to get here early for a seat on the terrace during the Henley Regatta in July. The Henley Regatta began in 1839 and received Royal patronage by Prince Albert in 1851. Henley staged the Olympic rowing events at both the 1908 and 1948 London Games.

TOP The Union Inn sign at Aylestone, Leicester, shows a working boat being gauged to assess the amount of tonnage it is carrying.

ABOVE The Eight Locks pub sign at Ryders Green in the heart of the Black Country.

RIGHT The Angel on the Bridge by the River Thames at Henley.

The Globe Inn at Linslade was originally called the Globe Beer Shop in 1841 and in later years provided stables for the boatmen's horses. The stables were converted to an extra bar in 1969. It has an attractive setting next to the canal as it passes through the wooded River Ouzel valley. The pub has become very popular in recent years and is festooned with flowers during the summer months.

BELOW The Globe Inn on the Grand Union Canal started as a beerhouse for the navvies when the canal was being dug.

In his book *Narrow Boat*, LTC Rolt describes the Cross Keys at Penkridge on the Staffs and Worcester Canal. This was during his epic voyage around the decaying canals in 1939. He described the pub as 'a little canal inn standing amid the fields beside the towpath waiting for boats that never came'. Mr Rolt would still have recognised the pub when this picture was taken in August 1978. Since then, the pub has considerably enlarged and has been engulfed by a housing estate. It is now a popular stopping place for visiting boaters.

ABOVE The Cross Keys at Penkridge.

RIGHT The Boat Inn's sign at Berkhamsted on the Grand Union Canal.

ABOVE The Barge Inn at Seend Cleeve in 1990. This very busy scene was taken shortly after the canal was reopened. It was a time when everyone who had a boat wanted to cruise the Kennet and Avon Canal. This beautiful navigation has now established itself as one of the most popular cruising waterways.

RIGHT The derelict Barge Inn by the equally derelict Kennet and Avon Canal in March 1973. The pub was reopened in time for the restoration of the canal in 1990. Fred Kempster, who was 8 feet 5 inches tall and Britain's tallest man, once lived at the Barge Inn around the time of the First World War.

Waterways in Winter

Icy conditions were a nightmare for the working boatman who had to cope with iced up canals and frozen locks. Self-employed boatmen were only paid on delivery of cargo, so being frozen up meant loss of income. The severe winter of 1963 ended regular commercial trading on the narrow canals.

ABOVE Boats ploughing through the ice in December 1981 at Denham on the Grand Union Canal.

RIGHT Somerton Deep Lock on the Oxford Canal. This section of the Oxford Canal is very open and exposed to wintry weather. It is likely that an ice-breaker would have worked on sections like these in the days of commercial trading in an effort to keep the canal open.

The Grand Union Canal was the main water highway between the Midland coalfields and the south. Delays in delivery because of freezing conditions meant customers would look elsewhere for supplies and so the canals lost trade to the more reliable railways.

ABOVE A frozen Tring Summit on the Grand Union Canal.

RIGHT Little Bedwyn on the Kennet and Avon Canal. This part of the canal is especially busy on Good Friday when the Devizes to Westminster canoe race passes here. On a bleak late afternoon in January, only dog walkers and the odd waterway photographer venture out on to the towpath.

Waterways Flora and Fauna

The annual ceremony of swan upping takes place on the Thames for six days on the first week in July. The purpose of swan upping is to mark all new cygnets with the same mark as their parents to ascertain ownership. On the Thames, the Queen shares ownership of mute swans with the Vintners' and Dyers' companies. The shared right of ownership was granted in the 15th century.

RIGHT A heron patiently waits for his dinner by the Grand Union Canal at Tring. The grey heron is one of Britain's largest waterside birds and is very common beside the rivers and canals of England and Wales. It prefers to hunt alone, standing motionless in shallow water, waiting for unwary fish to appear near the surface.

BELOW A swan admires its reflection in the River Thames.

ABOVE A cormorant poses in front of
Canary Wharf by the River Thames.
Cormorants, once a winter visitor to
the inland waterways, have become
common throughout the year,
especially on the River Thames.

151

LEFT Bird's-foot-trefoil is commonly called the 'egg and bacon' plant, because of its colours. It is a member of the pea family and is very common in coastal regions. The flowers in the picture are growing by the industrial Tame Valley Canal in the Black Country, a long way from the coast. A surprising variety of wild flowering plants can be found on the banks of Black Country canals.

BELOW This flourishing scene is not what one would expect to see by the Aire and Calder Navigation in such a dour place at Knottingley. Local people with permission from British Waterways have planted the towpath with flowers. The result is a startling floral display that would have been acceptable at any national flower show.

Into the 21st Century

Many big city canals went into decline during the mid-20th century and became rubbish-filled ditches. In many cases the public were denied access to the towpaths. Now, in the 21st century, people are actively encouraged to visit the canals. This has led to the construction of spectacular tubular steel footbridges like these at Castlefield, Manchester and Apsley on the Grand Union Canal.

RIGHT The Glaxo Building at the Great West Road, Brentford, has a long frontage by the Grand Union Canal.

OPPOSITE The Rolling Bridge outside Marks & Spencer's headquarters was the idea of British designer Thomas Heatherwick. The footbridge consists of eight triangular sections hinged at the walkway level that unfurls to approximately 40 feet high before curling up into an octagonal ball. A demonstration of the working bridge takes place at midday every Friday.

Modern office buildings built on old factory sites are appearing all over the canal system. Instead of wharves for transporting goods they landscape their waterside for the benefit of their workers and to enhance the appearance of the company.

Paddington Basin was one of the busiest places on the canals. A warehouse-flanked pool was crammed with boats loading and unloading coal, sand, timber and bricks. With the decline of waterborne traffic the basin fell into disuse and was closed off from the public. Now renamed Paddington Waterside, it became one of Europe's biggest urban regeneration schemes. There are offices, shops, restaurants, bars and hotels. New footpaths allow public access to the basin and its innovative bridges.

The former industrial area around the River Lea had become very run down before it was transformed into a central feature of the Olympic Park for the 2012 Olympic Games. A new lock was built and a number of new bridges span the waterways. The banks of the rivers were planted with wild flowers and now the Olympic Park is open free to visitors and has become an important recreational centre for East London. Passenger trip boats operate on the Waterworks River during the summer months.

The Lancaster Canal was an isolated waterway cut off from the rest of the system until the building of the Ribble Link in 2002. A small stream called the Savick Brook was canalised and made navigable by constructing a number of locks. This raised the new waterway from the River Ribble to the Lancaster Canal on the outskirts of Preston. Boats can now reach the Lancaster Canal via the Leeds and Liverpool Canal, the River Douglas and the River Ribble. The success of the Ribble Link has given hope to proposed new canals such as the Bedford and Grand Union Link to Milton Keynes which would provide an alternative route into the Fenland waterways.

ABOVE The Bow Back Rivers are a complex of waterways in East London formed by the River Lea before it reaches the River Thames. This section is now an important part of the new Olympic Park.

RIGHT A new section of the Lancaster Canal built for the Ribble Link near Preston.

The Falkirk Wheel is the world's first rotating boat lift and a masterpiece of modern engineering. Two counterbalanced water-filled caissons rotate within the wheel which uses gravity to keep the boats level. Only a tiny amount of electricity is required to get the operation started. The Falkirk Wheel provides the link between two restored canals reconnecting Glasgow and Edinburgh by water after years of dereliction. Opened in 2002, it has already become the second biggest tourist attraction in Scotland after Edinburgh Castle.

RIGHT AND BELOW The Falkirk Wheel Aqueduct carries boats from the top of the wheel to a tunnel underneath both the Antonine Wall and a railway. Then there are two locks raising boats to the Union Canal level. After that there are 32 lock-free miles all the way into Edinburgh.

Index

'*And when the evening mist clothes the riverside with poetry, as with a veil, the poor buildings lose themselves in the dim sky, and the tall chimneys become campanili, and the warehouses are palaces in the night*'.

JAMES WHISTLER
(1834–1903)